DESERT FOOTHILLS LIBRARY

DONATED BY

MR. & MRS. MARTIN FOLEY

The Romans

Denise Allard

Gareth Stevens Publishing
MILWAUKEE

For a free color catalog describing Gareth Stevens Publishing's list of high-quality books and multimedia programs, call 1-800-542-2595 (USA) or 1-800-461-9120 (Canada). Gareth Stevens Publishing's Fax: (414) 225-0377. See our catalog, too, on the World Wide Web: http://gsinc.com

Library of Congress Cataloging-in-Publication Data

Allard, Denise, 1952-
    The Romans / Denise Allard.
       p. cm. — (Pictures of the past)
    Includes index.
    Summary: Describes daily life in ancient Rome, discussing the home, shopping, farming, theater, sports, and religion.
    ISBN 0-8368-1716-8 (lib. bdg.)
    1. Rome—Civilization—Juvenile literature. [1. Rome—Civilization.]
    I. Title. II. Series: Pictures of the past (Milwaukee, Wis.)
    DG78.A55   1997
    937—dc21   96-46230

This edition first published in 1997 by
Gareth Stevens Publishing
1555 North RiverCenter Drive, Suite 201
Milwaukee, Wisconsin 53212 USA

Original © 1995 Zoë Books Limited, 15 Worthy Lane, Winchester, Hampshire, SO23 7AB, England. Additional end matter © 1997 by Gareth Stevens, Inc.

Illustrations: Harry Clow and Clive Spong

The publishers wish to acknowledge, with thanks, the DDA Photo Library for the use of the photograph on page 6.

Printed in the United States of America

1 2 3 4 5 6 7 8 9 01 00 99 98 97

Contents

Rome

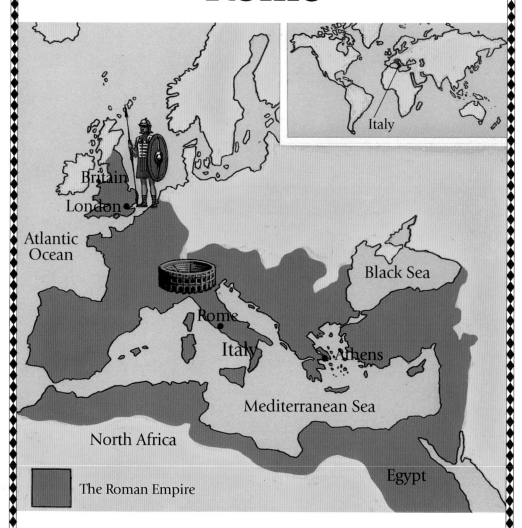

Italy

Britain

London

Atlantic
Ocean

Black Sea

Rome

Italy

Athens

Mediterranean Sea

North Africa

Egypt

The Roman Empire

The Romans ruled over all these lands.
Can you name the lands?

Rome

The city of Rome is beside the Tiber River in Italy. It is built on seven hills. Long ago, the Romans ruled many countries. These lands were called the Roman Empire.

Ancient Romans spoke a language called Latin. Latin words are sometimes still used today.

Long ago

The Colosseum in ancient Rome took eleven years to build.

Long ago

The Romans were good builders. They built this stadium called the Colosseum a long time ago. People went to the Colosseum to watch sports and games.

Researchers have learned about the ancient Romans from the objects the Romans left behind.

At home

This is the country home of a rich
Roman family.

At home

Family life was important to ancient Romans. The women ran the home. They brought up the children, and they made clothes. Rich families had people to cook and clean for them.

People who had money ate vegetables, fruits, fish, and other meats. They drank water and wine. Poor people ate mainly bread.

Children

Rich children went to school. Poor children had to work.

Children

In Roman families, grown-ups and children spent a lot of time together. Only rich children went to school. Boys spent more years in school than did girls. Poor children did not go to school at all.

At school, children learned how to read, write, and do "sums."

Town life

Each town had a forum, where there were shops and offices.

Town life

Ancient Romans built many
of their towns in the same
way. Each town had a
marketplace called a forum.
People lived in houses or
small apartments.

People in towns had jobs
making and selling goods.
They made and sold
pots, shoes, cloth, tools,
and furniture.

Shopping

The forum in each ancient Roman
town was a busy place.

Shopping

People bought goods at the marketplace. The shops opened onto the street. A sign showed what each shop was selling. Ancient Romans used coins for money.

The shopkeeper's family lived above the shop. The family often made the goods they sold.

Farming

Where do you think farmers went to
sell their products?

Farming

Most ancient Romans worked the land. Rich Romans owned big farms and large country houses. Other people did the work on the farm for the owner, who was often away.

Farmers grew fruits, vegetables, and grapes for wine. They also raised pigs, sheep, and cattle.

The baths

The Romans used oil, instead of soap, to clean themselves.

The baths

Ancient Roman towns had buildings where people could take a bath. First, they rubbed oil into their skin. Then they got into the water and scraped off the oil and dirt.

People also went to the baths to relax and meet friends. They played games and talked.

The theater

Pantomimes told a story through a
dancer and a chorus.

The theater

People loved going to the
theater on holidays. They
saw plays and listened to
music. They sat on stone
benches in the open air.
Actors wore costumes and
big masks.

Plays could be funny or sad.
Sometimes the plays were
in the form of pantomimes.

Races and games

There are many different kinds of
races today. Can you name some?

Races and games

The Romans liked going to
big stadiums. They cheered
the men who raced in chariots
pulled by horses. They also
watched men and animals
fight each other to the death.

There were four chariot teams
in ancient Rome. People
had their favorite. Winners
received prizes.

Soldiers

Soldiers of ancient Rome were
brave fighters.

Soldiers

The Romans ruled over many countries. Their army was well trained, and the soldiers made a good wage. Soldiers also built roads.

The army was made up of groups of soldiers called legions. Each troop of one hundred men was called a century.

Roads

The Roman army built new roads
wherever they went.

Roads

Ancient Roman roads went from one place to another by the shortest route. Some of these routes are still in use today.

When building a road, soldiers dug a trench and filled it with stones. The roads were designed to let rainwater drain away.

Forts

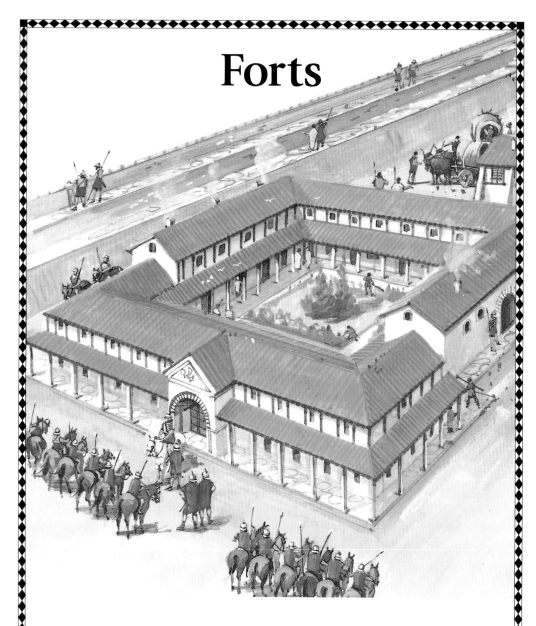

Strong walls were built around forts
to protect soldiers from attack.

Forts

When the Roman army took over a new land, the soldiers built forts there. The soldiers ate and slept inside these forts. They also stored weapons and food there.

Each Roman fort was built in the same way.

Gods and goddesses

Ancient Romans believed in many gods and goddesses.

Apollo: the god of the sun and music.

Ceres: the goddess of farming.

Diana: the goddess of the moon and hunting.

Hercules: the god of strength.

Juno: the goddess of women.

Jupiter: the king of the Roman gods.

Libitina: the goddess of death.

Mars: the god of war.

Mercury: the god who was the messenger for the gods.

Minerva: the goddess of wisdom, crafts, and trade.

Mithras: the god who looked after soldiers.

Neptune: the god of the sea.

Venus: the goddess of love and beauty.

Vesta: the goddess of the home and the fireside.

Vulcan: the god of fire.

Books

Ancient Rome. Simon James
(Viking Children's Books)

Greek and Roman Mythology A to Z. Kathleen Daly
(Facts on File)

Living in Ancient Rome. Odile Bombarde and
Claude Moatti (Forest House)

Rome in the Ancient World. Mike Corbishley
(Facts on File)

Videos

Claudius: Boy of Ancient Rome.
(Encyclopædia Britannica Educational Corp.)

Julius Caesar: The Rise of the Roman Empire.
(Encyclopædia Britannica Educational Corp.)

The Road to Ancient Rome. (Thomas S. Klise)

Web Sites

http://www.detour.com/~pkonin/

http://www.ed.gov/pubs/parents/History/
Home.html

Index